SAINT PADRE PIO [1]

Introduce your child to the inspiring life of Saint Padre Pio—filled with faith, miracles, and the love of Jesus!

In this beautifully illustrated and interactive 47-page Catholic children's book, young readers will journey through the heartwarming story of Saint Padre Pio, a humble Capuchin friar known for his deep prayer life, stigmata, and powerful miracles. Through gentle storytelling and illustrations, children will learn how Padre Pio became a friend of Jesus, a helper to the poor and sick, and a beloved saint who still prays for us from Heaven

More than just a storybook, this unique title also includes coloring pages—designed to engage children creatively while reinforcing the faith-filled messages. Perfect for bedtime reading, Sunday school, First Communion gifts, or Catholic classroom activities, Saint Padre Pio: The Flying Monk with Stigmata who loved Jesus is ideal for ages 2-12

This book inspires young hearts to trust in God, pray with love, and serve others joyfully—just like Padre Pio

Written, Designed and Published in the USA

For our dearest nephew Joel,

Your wonder lit the spark that shaped these pages,
Your questions whispered dreams through every line.
May the story of Saint Padre Pio guide many hearts,
And may your own forever shine.
Walk always in God's gentle light,
And share that light with the world—
Bright, brave, and full of grace.
With all our love,

Diya aunty and Joby uncle

Padre Pio- Francesco Forgione was born to
Orazio Forgione and Maria Giuseppa Di Nunzio,
peasant farmers in Pietrelcina, Italy on May 25,
1887. His parents entrusted their newborn to
the protection of St. Francis of Assisi, naming
him Francesco

The family was devoutly Catholic, attending daily Mass, praying the Rosary, and abstaining from meat three times a week.He was baptized in the Santa Anna Chapel and later became an altar server there

At age five, Francesco consecrated himself to Jesus. He had visions and conversations with Jesus, Mary, and his guardian angel. He experienced both heavenly visions and attacks from the devil

At age of five Francesco experienced a vision of Sacred Heart of Jesus. In this vision Lord placed his hand on Francesco's head and promised St Francis that the boy would remain faithful to him

Like other children in Pietrelcina, Francesco spent much of his childhood helping his family. When his parents deemed him old enough, they entrusted him with two sheep to tend along with other young shepherds

Francisco's mother always wrapped his meal in a clean napkin so when he stopped to eat, he would sit on the ground carefully and fold the napkin on his lap, glance around and then look upward before eating with reverence. If a crumble fell he would pick it up kiss it eat it -a sign of respect for bread which he called the "grace of God"

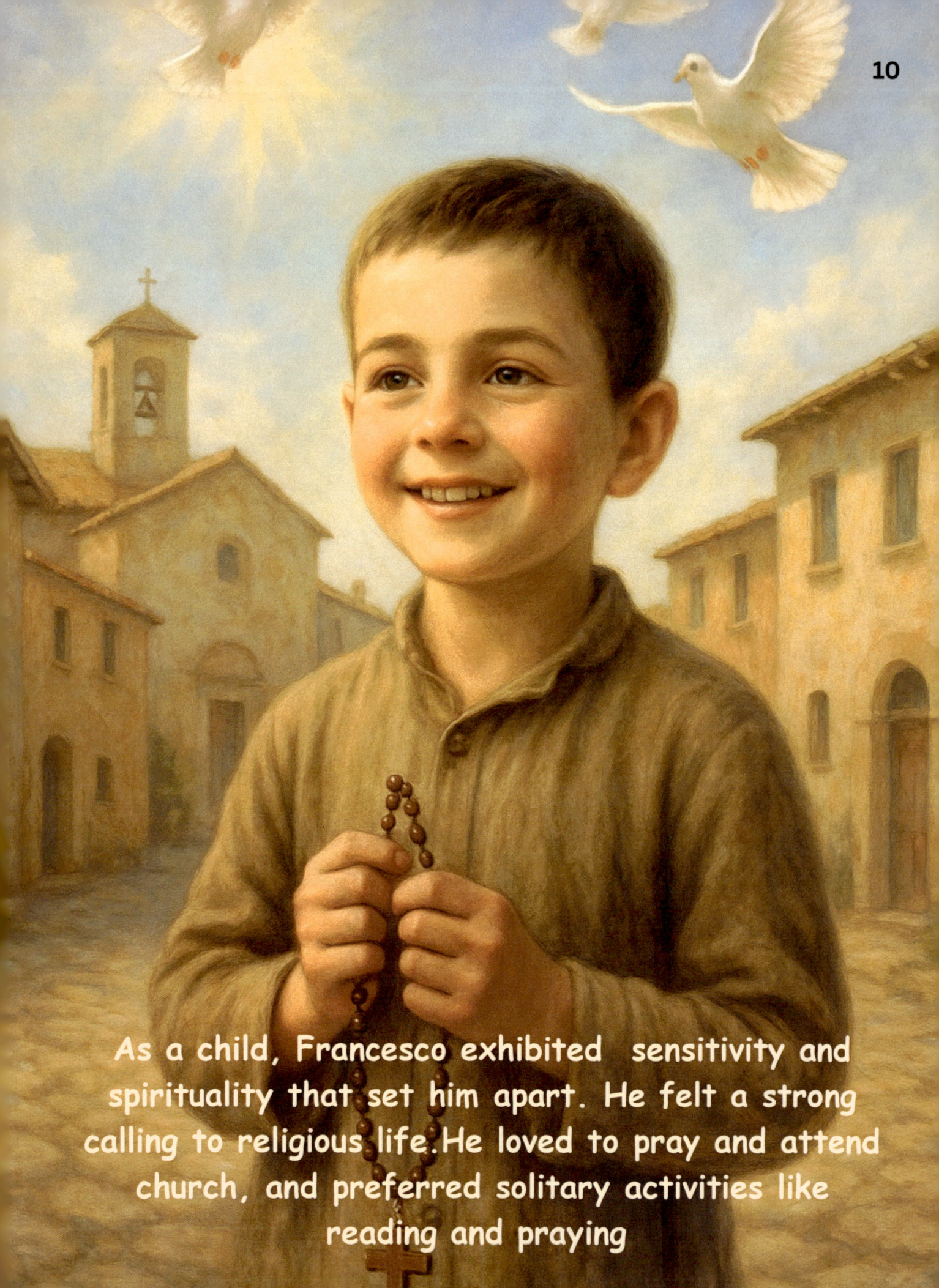

As a child, Francesco exhibited sensitivity and spirituality that set him apart. He felt a strong calling to religious life.He loved to pray and attend church, and preferred solitary activities like reading and praying

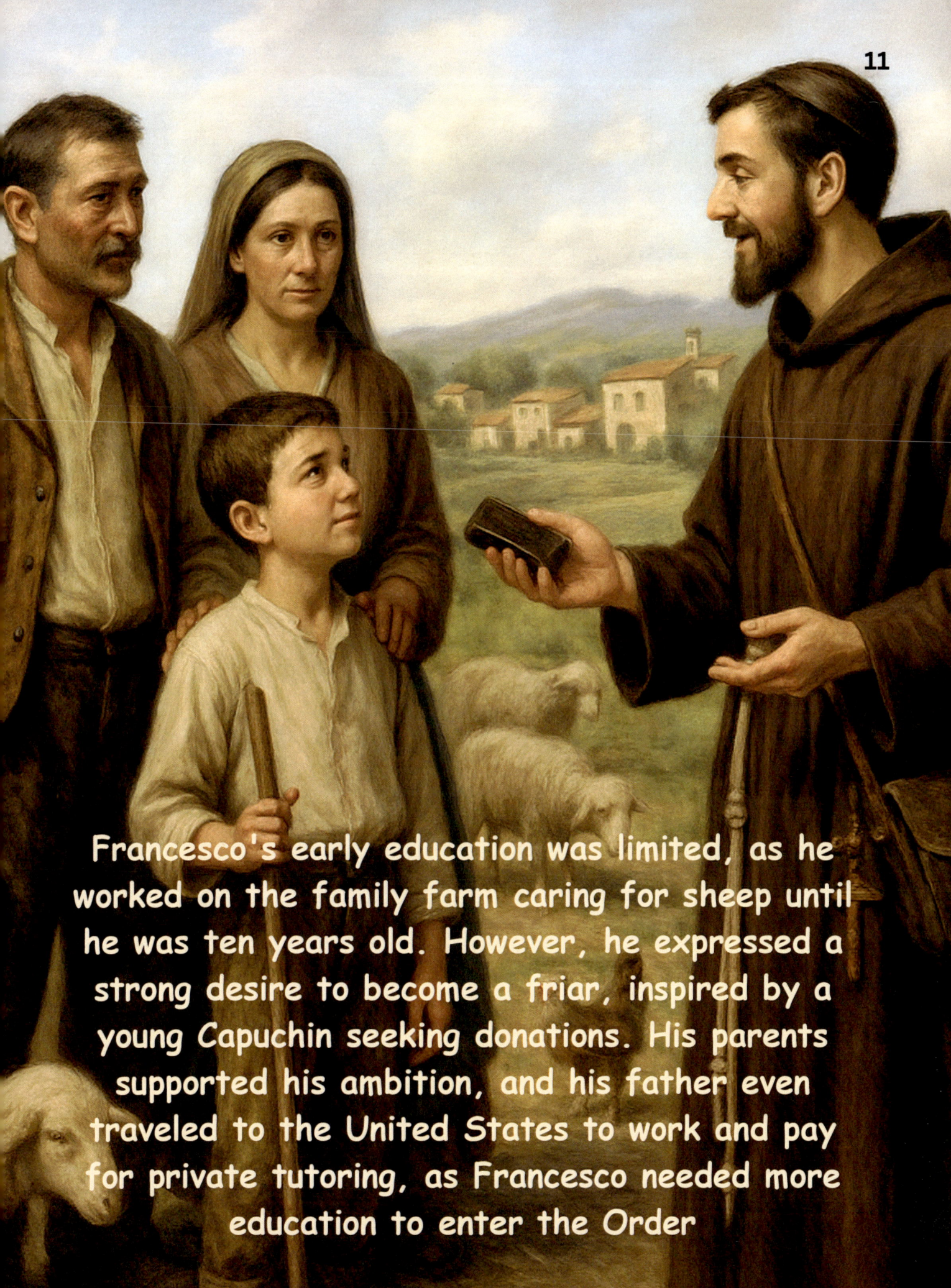

Francesco's early education was limited, as he worked on the family farm caring for sheep until he was ten years old. However, he expressed a strong desire to become a friar, inspired by a young Capuchin seeking donations. His parents supported his ambition, and his father even traveled to the United States to work and pay for private tutoring, as Francesco needed more education to enter the Order

At fifteen, he joined the Capuchin Order in Morcone, Italy

On August 10th 1910 in the Cathedral of Benevento, Francesco Forgione was ordained as a priest. On August 14th 1910, he celebrated his first solemn Mass at the parish church of Pietrelcina. That day marked the beginning of a ministry full of grace

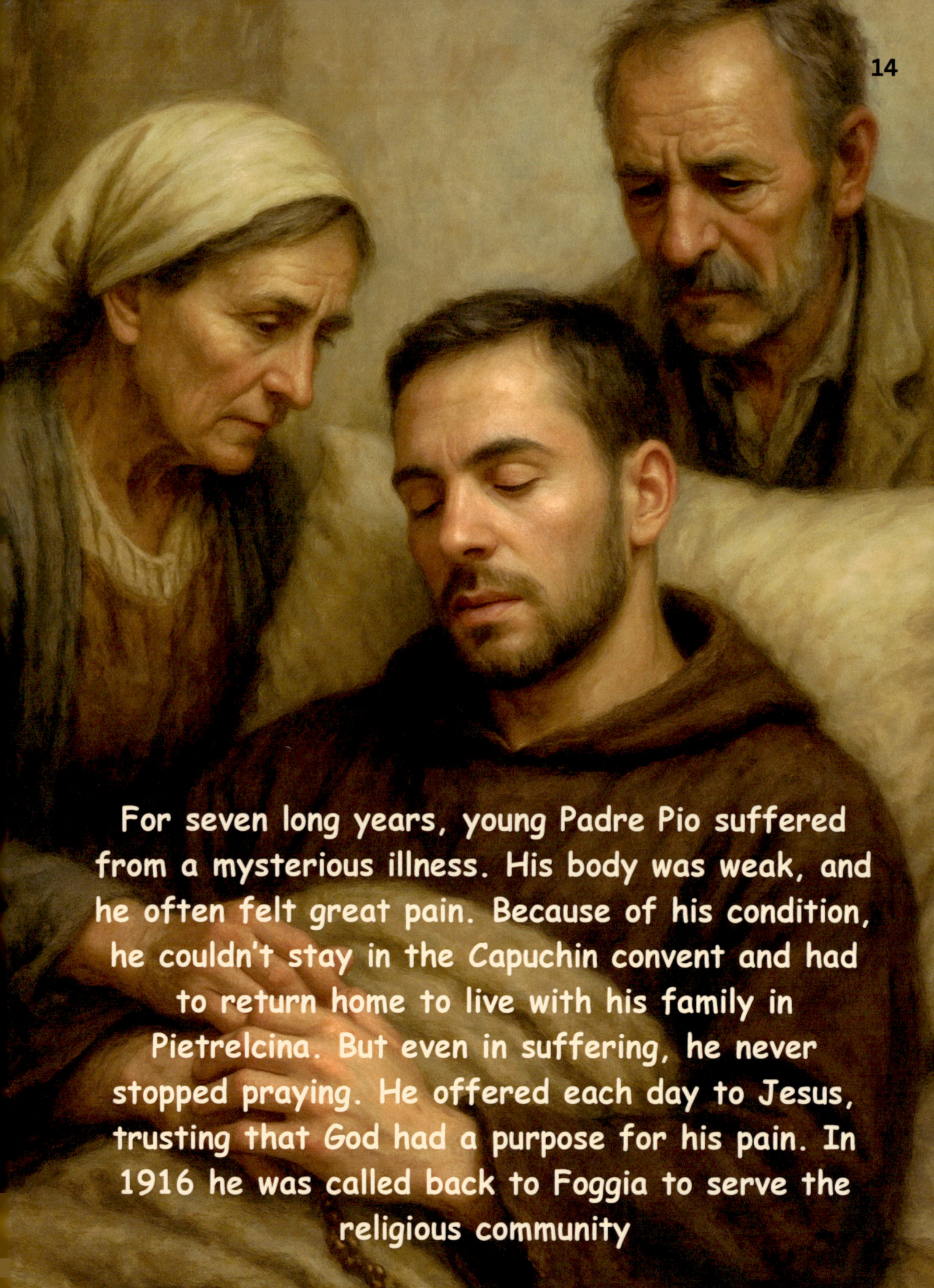

For seven long years, young Padre Pio suffered from a mysterious illness. His body was weak, and he often felt great pain. Because of his condition, he couldn't stay in the Capuchin convent and had to return home to live with his family in Pietrelcina. But even in suffering, he never stopped praying. He offered each day to Jesus, trusting that God had a purpose for his pain. In 1916 he was called back to Foggia to serve the religious community

One day, Padre Pio was praying quietly in the church when something amazing happened—his hands began to glow, and marks appeared, just like the wounds of Jesus

His hands, feet, and side had small red marks—
just like Jesus had on the cross!
 The Mysterious Wounds
These special marks are called stigmata. They
looked like little wounds and would sometimes hurt,
but Padre Pio didn't complain. He smiled and said,
"These are a gift. I want to offer my pain to
Jesus to help others." He wore mittens to cover
his hands so no one would notice. He didn't want
attention—he only wanted to love and pray

Padre Pio's life was shaped by long hours of prayer and constant self-discipline. His letters to his spiritual directors unveil the ineffable suffering—both physical and spiritual—that accompanied him throughout his years. They also reveal his profound union with God and his burning love for the Blessed Eucharist and Our Blessed Lady

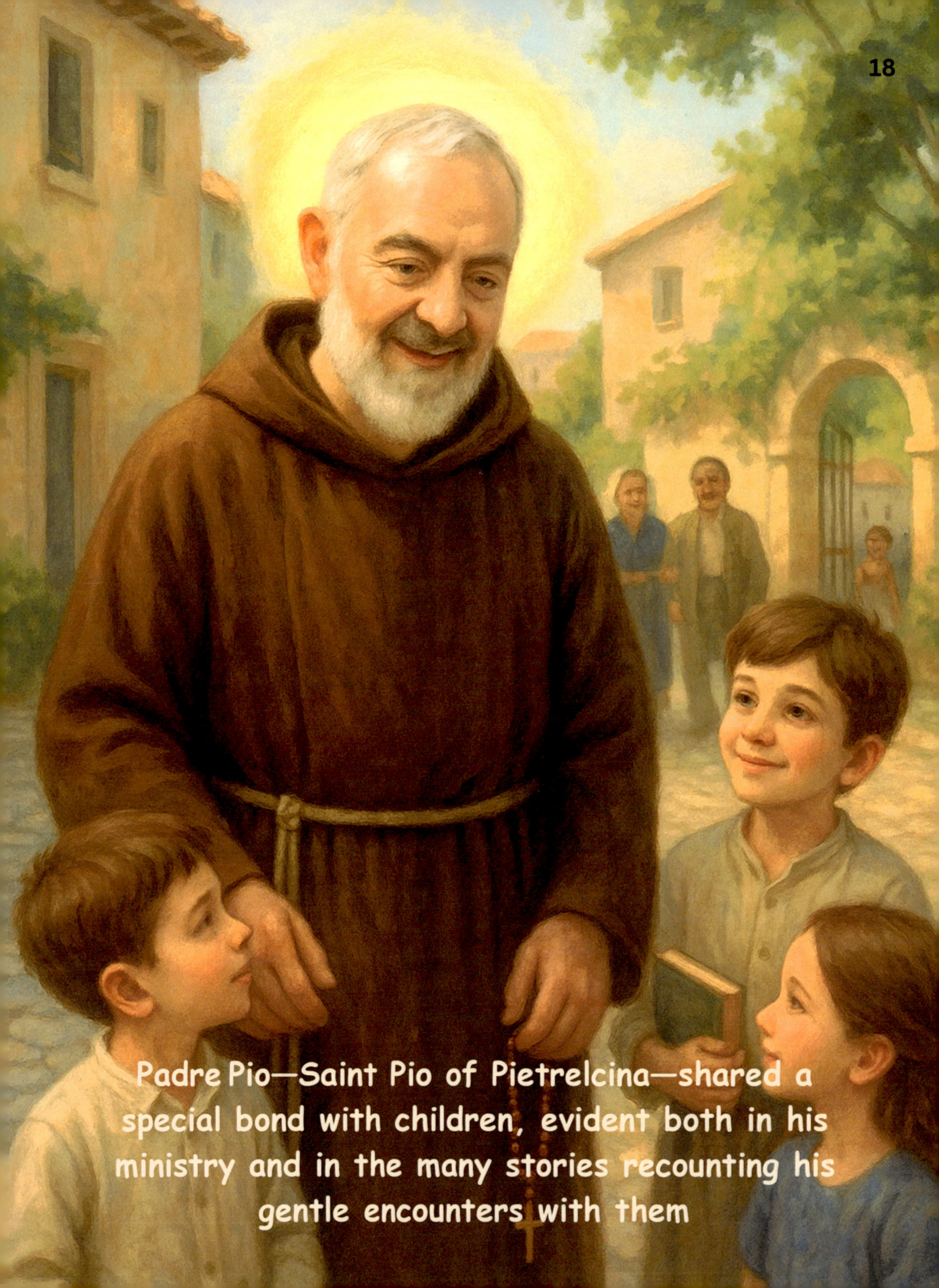

Padre Pio—Saint Pio of Pietrelcina—shared a special bond with children, evident both in his ministry and in the many stories recounting his gentle encounters with them

Padre Pio spent his days praying, helping the sick, and teaching people about God's love. His church was always full, because everyone felt at peace when he prayed

While hearing confessions, the saint often smelled the fragrance of flowers as sins were revealed. Some penitents waited up to two weeks for their turn in his confessional. Padre Pio could also read the hearts of penitents, gently reminding them of sins they had forgotten or omitted

Padre Pio could do something no one expected—
bilocate. He could be in two places at once!
Sometimes people saw him far away even though
he had never left the monastery

And once, a fellow friar saw something truly miraculous—Padre Pio flying through the air, arms outstretched like a bird, on his way to help someone in need!

During World War II, Allied bomber crews based in Puglia (southern Italy) were assigned bombing runs on the town of San Giovanni Rotondo, home to Padre Pio

Numerous pilots recounted seeing a friar in brown robes appear before their aircraft, gesturing to turn away. Suddenly, their bombs malfunctioned, doors opened, and planes aborted their missions—without any action from the crew

People called him the Flying Monk. He is renowned for experiencing levitation as one of several supernatural gifts.One account describes him rising to the height of the pulpit during a religious ceremony, according to Miracles of the Saints

Before bedtime, children would whisper, "Padre Pio, pray for me!" And he would. Even now, in Heaven, he listens to every prayer

Padre Pio died peacefully on September 23, 1968, at the age of 81

Years after he died, the Church wanted to move Padre Pio's body to a new resting place, so more people could visit and pray. When they opened his coffin in 2008—40 years later—they were shocked! His body had not decayed the way most bodies do. "Incorrupt" means that God protected Padre Pio's body from breaking down like usual. Today, if you visit San Giovanni Rotondo, you can see Padre Pio's body lying in a beautiful glass case. He looks peaceful, like he's just sleeping

Dear Saint Padre Pio, Help me to love Jesus like you did, To pray every day, And to always help others. Amen

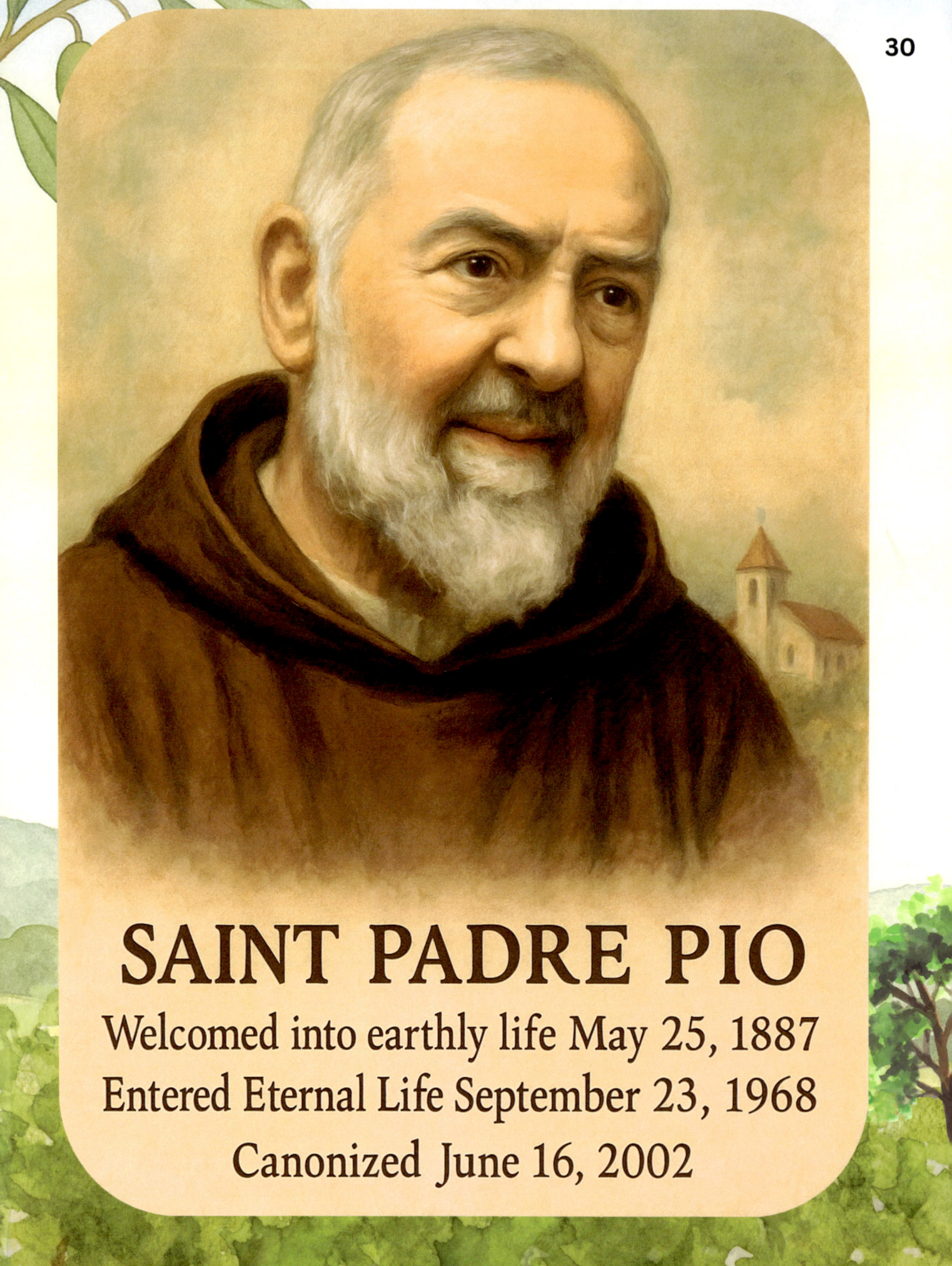

SAINT PADRE PIO
Welcomed into earthly life May 25, 1887
Entered Eternal Life September 23, 1968
Canonized June 16, 2002

MY PADRE PIO COLORING BOOK

PADRE PIO'S HOMELAND

Padre Pio grew up in Italy—
a boot-shaped country
far across the sea.

HEALING BLESSING

COLOR-BY-NUMBER ROSARY

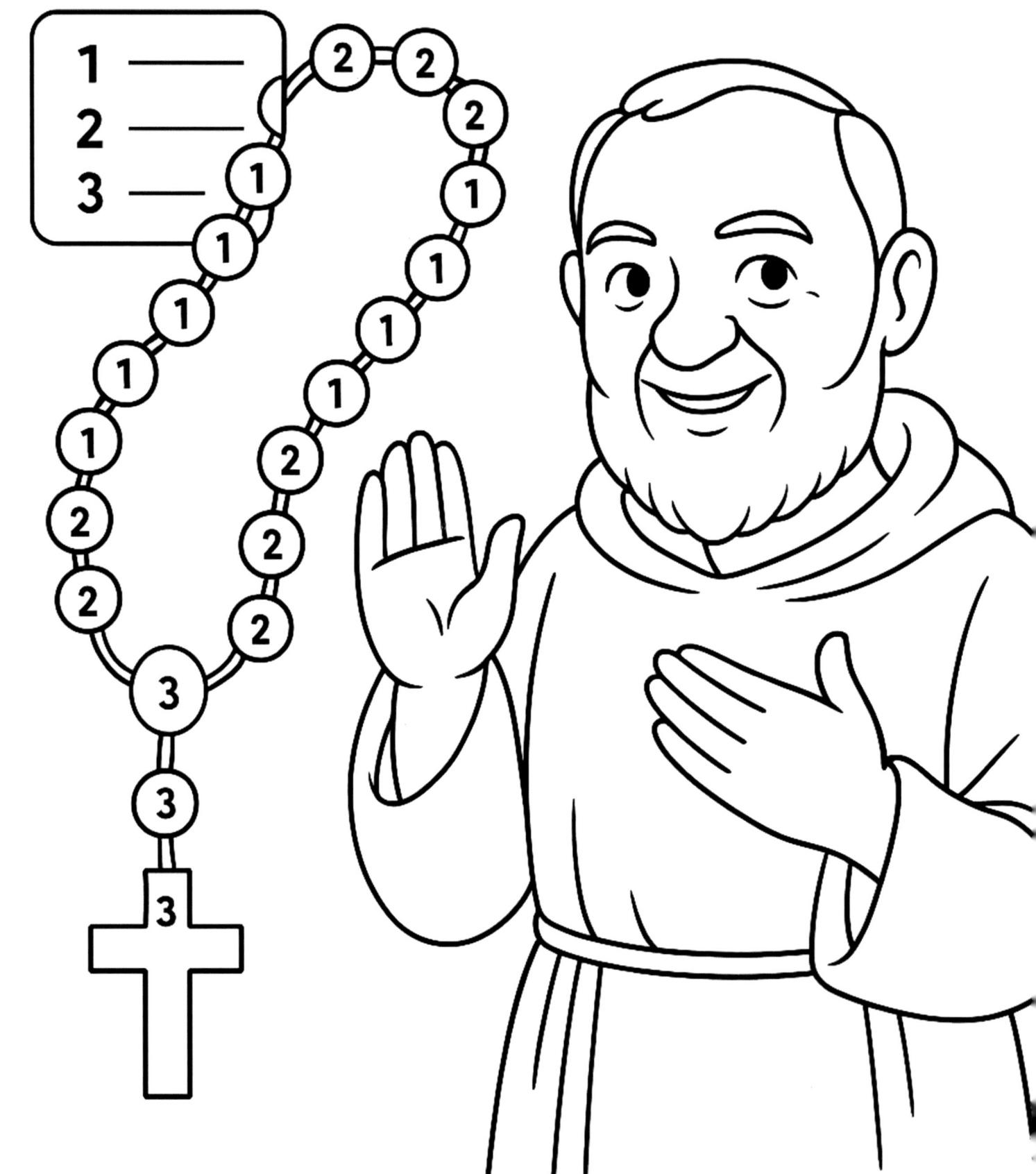

KIND CONFESSOR

VISITS THE SICK

STIGMATA OF LOVE

PATH TO PRAYER

THE FLYING MONK

Certificate of Completion

This certifies that

_____

has joyfully completed the
Saint Padre Pio Coloring Adventure!

May Saint Padre Pio inspire you to pray, be kind,
and share God's love.

_____
Signature

_____
Date

Dr. Diya Abraham, Ph.D

A researcher at heart and mentor by calling, Dr. Diya Abraham earned her doctorate in Neuroscience from the Max Planck Institute in Germany and completed a post-doctoral fellowship at the University of California, San Francisco. Her work on circadian rhythms—the genes that keep our inner clocks in sync—has appeared in leading peer-reviewed journals and has been showcased on international conference stages

Dr. Abraham weaves science into faith-infused learning experiences. Through Bee Little Curious, the company she founded to enrich curious minds & soul, she creates evidence-based educational resources and uplifting religious products. She partners with parish schools to embed STEM principles into grace-filled curricula. Saint Padre Pio—the inaugural title in her forthcoming series on the saints will nurture young minds and honor the heroes of the Church

Joby James

Joby James has built an illustrious career at the intersection of engineering, enterprise-class cybersecurity sales and tech entrepreneurship. As the founder of cybersecurity firm, his team helps companies safeguard data while equipping organizations to navigate the digital world safely and responsibly

Joby believes that safeguarding souls matters just as much as protecting systems—a conviction nurtured through years of mentoring youth groups, where he first shared the saint stories that now inspire his writing. In this inaugural title Saint Padre Pio, he blends his business acumen with a catechetical heart

Enquiries: info@beelittlecurious.com

www.ingramcontent.com/pod-product-compliance
Lightning Source LLC
Chambersburg PA
CBRC090828120626
46547CB00008B/630